GRADE 3

Language Arts Activities Using Colorful Cut-Outs™

BY JOYCE KOHFELDT AND JOHNNY WARRICK

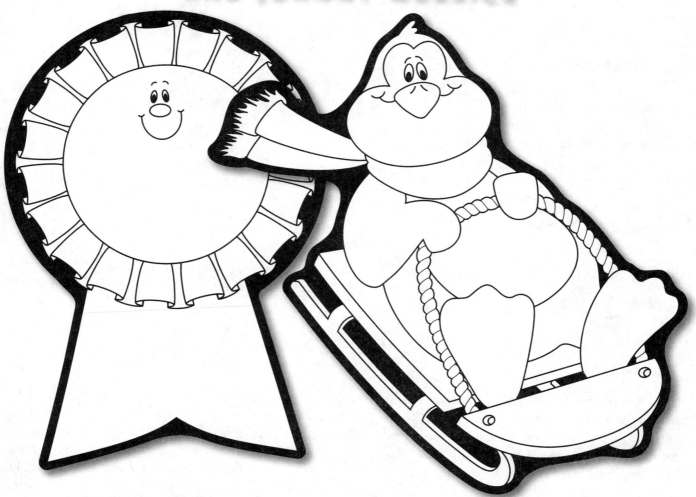

Carson-Dellosa Publishing Company, Inc. • Greensboro, North Carolina

Dedications

I dedicate this book to my mom, Doris Kohfeldt,
who has always been there to support my professional activities,
and to Jake Converse, a super lifetime learner.—Joyce Kohfeldt

I dedicate this book to all of the students whom I have taught.
They always inspire me to make learning an exciting and hands-on experience
that helps them become better problem solvers.—Johnny Warrick

Credits

Editors: Ashley Anderson and Cari Jackson
Layout Design: Lori Jackson
Cover Design: Peggy Jackson
Cover Illustration: Erik Huffine

This book has been correlated to state, national, and Canadian provincial standards. Visit *www.carsondellosa.com* to search for and view its correlations to your standards.

ISBN 978-1-60022-043-2

Table of Contents

Introduction

Welcome to *Language Arts Activities Using Colorful Cut-Outs*™!

Within this book, there are more than 40 activities that will help students practice important language arts skills while interacting with each other. Not only will students have fun doing the activities in this book, but they will also learn. *Language Arts Activities Using Colorful Cut-Outs*™ includes activities that focus on using different verb tenses, solving analogies, editing, building words with prefixes and suffixes, using good vocabulary, putting words in alphabetical order, identifying parts of speech, and many more. A Skills Matrix (pages 9–10) has been included so that teachers can easily correlate the skills in each activity to daily classroom lessons.

Teachers will enjoy the easy preparation and minimal supplies required. Each easy-to-assemble activity uses sturdy Colorful Cut-Outs™ that will motivate and actively engage students. Carson-Dellosa's Colorful Cut-Outs™ are available in a variety of shapes and themes so that teachers can tailor each activity to their classroom needs. This book also includes several reproducible cut-outs to enlarge and copy on sturdy, colorful card stock. Reproducible cut-outs can be used for any of the activities in this book or as take-home pieces to encourage students to practice challenging skills outside the classroom. Easy assembly instructions and step-by-step activity directions are provided for each activity, and the durable cut-outs can be used over and over again, year after year. The activities in this book are versatile and easy to use for any classroom need—whole-group, small-group, centers, or take-home practice.

Organization

Language Arts Activities Using Colorful Cut-Outs™ was written with the busy classroom teacher in mind. In addition to the easy reference of the skills matrix, each type of activity in this book is coded with an icon (see box), and many of the activities include three different levels of difficulty from which to choose. Students can use the novice level cards (each coded with a ●) when they are starting a new skill, the apprentice level cards (each coded with a ▲) as they gain confidence, and the expert level cards (each coded with a ■) when they are ready for a challenge. In many cases, the cards can be mixed together to expand the activity and include more students. The icon on each activity card makes it quick and easy to sort the cards into levels after using them together. Teachers can also prepare a set of cards for each level and keep them separated for leveled centers.

Activity Icons

- Bag It Activities
- Hot Potato Activities
- Living Lineup Activities
- Attribute Bag It Activities
- Toss It Activities
- Search Activities

Preparation and Materials

Most of the activities in this book require nothing more than a set of Colorful Cut-Outs™ and a copy machine. Each Bag It activity also requires one colorful gift bag. (You can use a simple brown paper bag instead; however, a handled gift bag is more festive, sturdier, and can be easily transported throughout the room.) Each Toss It activity requires one or two large cubes—either inflatable cubes or homemade cubes using the directions on page 8. Almost all additional required supplies are items that teachers already have, such as pencils, paper, and resealable plastic bags.

When preparing an activity, simply copy the activity cards, cut them apart, and attach them to the cut-outs. If desired, laminate and cut out the assembled cut-outs for extra durability. Store them according to the directions provided.

Variations

Before beginning any activity, explain the directions and practice a few examples with students. When students understand the activity, it can be adapted for whole-group, small-group, or center lessons, depending on classroom needs. For whole-group activities, have students work in pairs or groups of three so that more students can be involved in each round. Or, where possible, divide students into small groups and encourage them to work together to complete each activity. The activities in this book are perfect for center use and encourage independent learning because answers are printed on the right-hand side of each activity card when there is a definite answer available. (Some activities ask for students' opinions, so answers will vary.)

Evaluation and Assessment

Evaluating students' needs and assessing their skill mastery is easy with the pretests and posttests that are provided in this book. Before beginning an activity, make copies of the pretest and posttest for each student and cut them apart. Give students time to take the pretest and encourage them to do their best even if they are not sure about an answer or how to complete a task. Then, have students complete the activity. Repeat as needed to allow students to practice the skill. (*Note:* The activities in this book are not intended to teach skills, only to provide skill practice. Students may need additional instruction.) After students have practiced the skill using the activity and additional lessons as needed, administer the posttest. If some students still struggle with the skill, prepare a take-home version of the activity so that students can practice at home. If several students are still struggling, repeat the activity on another day so that students can continue group practice.

Activity Tips

Take-Home Activities

Reproducible cut-outs have been provided so that multiple sets of activity cards can be made for take-home practice. Whenever students need extra practice with a skill, prepare a set of take-home cut-outs for each student using enlarged copies of the Bonus Cut-Outs (pages 106–109). Make a copy of the activity instructions and send home the prepared cut-outs. Include a copy of the Family Letter (page 11) and any additional specific notes to explain the exciting lessons that students are learning each day. Families will enjoy being included in their children's learning process, and students will benefit from the extra practice.

Bag It Activities

Bag It activities focus on interactive learning. Students are often asked to work with classmates to accomplish a task or verify an answer, so cooperation skills are also a focus of Bag It activities. In addition to Colorful Cut-Outs™, each Bag It activity requires a colorful gift bag with handles (available at most craft stores). Teachers may choose to use a paper lunch bag, but a gift bag is sturdier and the handles make it easier for students to pass around the room during use. The bag will also serve as storage for the activity when it is not in use.

Hot Potato Activities

Hot Potato activities are a variation of the classic game. Students sit in a circle and quickly pass cut-outs to their classmates. Instead of having only one item to pass like the traditional game, every student is holding a cut-out. When the teacher signals to stop, each student will turn over the cut-out that he is holding. Students with programmed cut-outs will then take turns reading them and leading the class in completing the activity.

Living Lineup Activities

Living Lineup activities focus on forming lines based on specific directions. In one activity, students will form lines to put words in alphabetical order. In another activity, students will form lines based on whether they can compose sentences using words as different parts of speech. Living Lineup activities are perfect practice for developing teamwork and cooperation skills, as well as written and oral communication skills.

Attribute Bag It Activities

Attribute Bag It activities are like regular Bag It activities, but they focus on describing attributes of items or cut-outs. In one activity, students will look at similar Colorful Cut-Outs™ and sort them by common attributes. In another activity, students will look at items and describe their attributes, such as shape, size, texture, and color. Like regular Bag It activities, each Attribute Bag It activity requires a colorful gift bag with handles in addition to a set of Colorful Cut-Outs™.

Toss It Activities

Toss It activities focus on matching and comparing skills. Students will roll large cubes and compare the results of each roll to the cut-outs that they are holding. Toss It activities are best for small-group or center activities but can be adapted for whole-group use if a teacher rolls the cubes and announces the results to all students. Inflatable cubes can be purchased and reused for several Toss It activities if the cut-outs are laminated and attached with removable tape or hook-and-loop tape. Cubes can also be constructed following the directions and illustrations on page 8.

Search Activities

Search activities focus on knowing basic facts and terms. Each student will hold a cut-out that has two sentences on it. One student will have a "Start Card" that is identified by an icon. That student will start the activity by reading her cut-out. (The answer is printed on the right-hand side of each cut-out, but students should not read answers aloud. They are provided only for self-checking purposes.) The student who has the answer to the question will respond by reading his cut-out. The activity continues until all of the cut-outs have been read and the student with the start card reads the final answer. (Because cut-outs must be read in a specific order, the levels of Search activities cannot be mixed together like the levels of the other types of activities.) As skills improve, students can be encouraged to complete each round faster than the previous round. Because Search activities are self-checking, they are excellent for student-guided small-group practice or center use.

Cube Assembly

MATERIALS: two clean, empty, large juice cartons; ruler; pencil; scissors; newspaper; wide tape; solid-colored wrapping paper (optional)

1. Measure the width of the bottom of one carton. Draw a line on the side of each carton so that the height is the same as the width of the base. Cut along each line to remove the tops of the cartons.

2. Stuff one carton bottom with newspaper to add stability.

3. Slide the stuffed carton bottom inside the empty carton bottom to create a cube. (If needed, bend the edges of the stuffed carton bottom somewhat to make it fit.)

4. Tape around the edges to hold the cube together. If desired, wrap the cube with solid-colored wrapping paper to cover the juice labels.

Note: Some Colorful Cut-Outs™ will not fit on the sides of a juice carton. Consider using the Bonus Cut-Out Patterns in the back of this book as an alternative if you do not have a set of appropriately sized cut-outs.

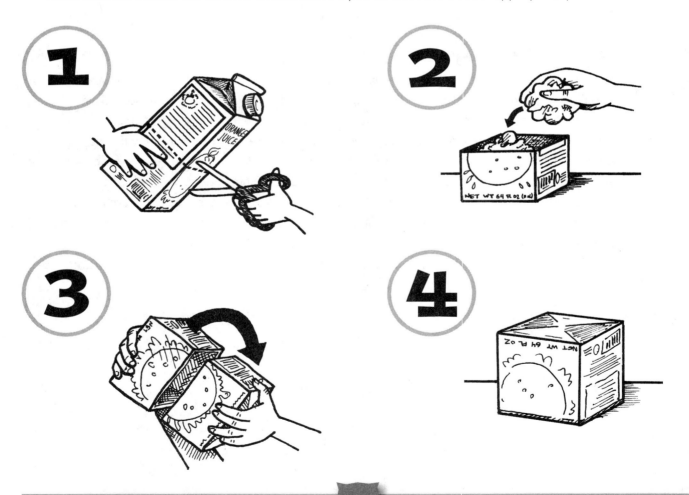

Skills Matrix

Activity Titles / Skills	1 Words That Sound the Same	2 What Does Not Belong?	3 More Than One Meaning	4 Using Verb Tenses	5 Solving Analogies	6 Editing for Conventions	7 Sentence Roundup	8 Counting Syllables	9 How Do You Spell the Plural?	10 Focus on Word Choice	11 Be an Expert: Alphabetical Order	12 Be an Expert: It's a Noun and a Verb
Editing for Conventions						☆						
Analogies					☆							
Verb Tense				☆								
Plurals					☆				☆			
Parts of Speech										☆		☆
Prefixes/Suffixes												
Syllabication								☆				
Alphabetical Order											☆	
Homonyms	☆		☆									
Synonyms/Antonyms					☆					☆		
Compound Words												
Vocabulary	☆	☆	☆		☆					☆		☆
Concept Development		☆			☆							
Attributes/Categorization		☆			☆							
Sentence Structure	☆			☆			☆					☆
Reading Comprehension												
Fact vs. Opinion												
Listening Comprehension	☆	☆	☆		☆		☆	☆		☆		
Written and Oral Language Conventions	☆			☆			☆		☆			☆

Skills Matrix

Activity Titles	13	14	15	16	17	18	19	20	21	22	23
Skills	Comparing and Contrasting	Using Your Senses	Adding Variety	Prefixes	Suffixes	Synonyms	Antonyms	Compound Words	What Does It Mean?	Blended Words	Fact or Opinion?
Editing for Conventions											
Analogies											
Verb Tense											
Plurals											
Parts of Speech											
Prefixes/Suffixes				☆	☆						
Syllabication											
Alphabetical Order											
Homonyms											
Synonyms/Antonyms						☆	☆				
Compound Words								☆			
Vocabulary		☆	☆	☆	☆	☆	☆	☆	☆	☆	
Concept Development		☆									
Attributes/ Categorization	☆	☆									
Sentence Structure			☆								
Reading Comprehension			☆								☆
Fact vs. Opinion											☆
Listening Comprehension			☆			☆	☆	☆	☆	☆	☆
Written and Oral Language Conventions	☆	☆	☆								

_7-6-11_
(date)

Dear Family,

    This year, I will learn many new language arts skills at school. I will learn to solve analogies. I will put words in alphabetical order. I will also practice identifying parts of speech.

    I will learn many things about becoming a good writer. My class will practice editing the stories that we read. I will edit for apostrophes, commas, quotation marks, ending punctuation, and correct spelling when reviewing sentences and dialogue. I will also learn to use different verb tenses.

    I will learn so many new things that I just can't wait to show you. You can help me at home, too. I will be bringing home some fun activities that we can do together. The more I practice, the faster I will be able to master new skills.

    Thank you for taking the time to help me practice new language arts skills.

Love,

Hayden

Words That Sound the Same

Programming Instructions

Three levels of activity cards have been provided. In each level, students are required to spell homophones and then use each word in a sentence to show understanding of the definitions. The levels increase in difficulty from the Novice Level (page 13) to the Expert Level (page 15). Select an activity level. For a challenge, mix the levels together. Copy and cut apart the activity cards and attach each one to the front of a Colorful Cut-Out™. Decorate the front of a colorful gift bag with an extra cut-out from the set and attach the Bag It! Label (page 13, 14, or 15). Copy and cut out the activity directions (below) and attach them to the back of the bag. Place the cut-outs inside the bag. Assess students' skill mastery using the Pretest and Posttest (page 16).

Objectives

Students will spell homophones and use the words in sentences in order to show understanding of the definitions.

Activity Directions

1. Shuffle the programmed cut-outs and place them in the bag.
2. Have a student take a cut-out from the bag and read it aloud slowly two times. (Remind students not to spell the words when they read them aloud.)
3. Each student should take a moment to think about the words and whisper his answers to a neighbor.
4. The student who selected the cut-out should choose a classmate to answer aloud. Other students should each show a thumbs-up if they agree. The student who selected the cut-out should confirm the correct spellings.
5. Set aside the cut-out and let another student take a turn. The activity continues until all of the cut-outs have been used or all students have taken turns.
6. When the activity is complete, store the cut-outs in the bag.

Teacher Note: When students compose sentences, confirm appropriate word usage as needed.

Words That Sound the Same

1. One student should take a cut-out from the bag and read it aloud slowly two times.
2. Each student should take a moment to think about the words and whisper his answers to a neighbor.
3. The student who selected the cut-out should choose a classmate to answer aloud. Other students should each show a thumbs-up if they agree. The student who is holding the cut-out should confirm the correct spellings.
4. The student should set aside the cut-out and pass the bag to another student to take a turn. The activity continues until all of the cut-outs have been used or all students have taken turns.
5. When the activity is complete, store the cut-outs in the bag.

Words That Sound the Same

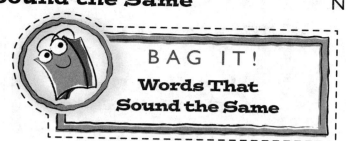

BAG IT!

Words That Sound the Same

Spell *hole* and *whole*. Use each word in a sentence.

Spell *sail* and *sale*. Use each word in a sentence.

Spell *cell* and *sell*. Use each word in a sentence.

Spell *made* and *maid*. Use each word in a sentence.

Spell *I* and *eye*. Use each word in a sentence.

Spell *deer* and *dear*. Use each word in a sentence.

Spell *be* and *bee*. Use each word in a sentence.

Spell *one* and *won*. Use each word in a sentence.

Spell *meet* and *meat*. Use each word in a sentence.

Spell *for* and *four*. Use each word in a sentence.

Spell *see* and *sea*. Use each word in a sentence.

Spell *to*, *too*, and *two*. Use each word in a sentence.

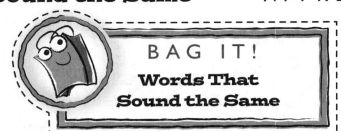

BAG IT!

Words That Sound the Same

Spell *no* and *know*.
Use each word in
a sentence.

Spell *bear* and *bare*.
Use each word in
a sentence.

Spell *ate* and *eight*.
Use each word in
a sentence.

Spell *right* and *write*.
Use each word in
a sentence.

Spell *by* and *buy*.
Use each word in
a sentence.

Spell *sum* and *some*.
Use each word in
a sentence.

Spell *here* and *hear*.
Use each word in
a sentence.

Spell *beet* and *beat*.
Use each word in
a sentence.

Spell *plain* and *plane*.
Use each word in
a sentence.

Spell *toe* and *tow*.
Use each word in
a sentence.

Spell *red* and *read*.
Use each word in
a sentence.

Spell *not* and *knot*.
Use each word in
a sentence.

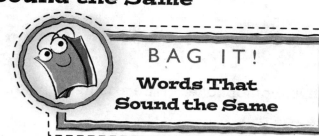

BAG IT!

**Words That
Sound the Same**

■ Spell *way* and *weigh*.
Use each word in
a sentence.

■ Spell *threw* and *through*.
Use each word in
a sentence.

■ Spell *peace* and *piece*.
Use each word in
a sentence.

■ Spell *its* and *it's*.
Use each word in
a sentence.

■ Spell *steal* and *steel*.
Use each word in
a sentence.

■ Spell *flour* and *flower*.
Use each word in
a sentence.

■ Spell *blew* and *blue*.
Use each word in
a sentence.

■ Spell *groan* and *grown*.
Use each word in
a sentence.

■ Spell *hair* and *hare*.
Use each word in
a sentence.

■ Spell *your* and *you're*.
Use each word in
a sentence.

■ Spell *night* and *knight*.
Use each word in
a sentence.

■ Spell *there, their,*
and *they're*.
Use each word in
a sentence.

Name: _____ Date: _____

Read each word and write its homophone. Write a sentence with each word.

1. nose _____

_____

_____

2. weak _____

_____

_____

✂ -

Name: _____ Date: _____

Words That Sound the Same Posttest

Read each word and write its homophone. Write a sentence with each word.

1. waist _____

_____

_____

2. tail _____

_____

_____

What Does Not Belong?

Programming Instructions

Two levels of activity cards have been provided. In each level, students are required to listen to lists of items and determine which item does not belong in the group. Students will also explain why the items do not belong. The levels increase in difficulty from the Apprentice Level (page 18) to the Expert Level (page 19). Select an activity level. For a challenge, mix the levels together. Copy and cut apart the activity cards and attach each one to the front of a Colorful Cut-Out™. Decorate the front of a colorful gift bag with an extra cut-out from the set and attach the Bag It! Label (page 18 or 19). Copy and cut out the activity directions (below) and attach them to the back of the bag. Place the cut-outs inside the bag. Assess students' skill mastery using the Pretest and Posttest (page 20).

Objective

Students will use categorization and reasoning skills to determine what does not belong in lists of items and why.

Activity Directions

1. Divide the class into small groups of 3–4 students.
2. Shuffle the cut-outs and place them in the bag.
3. Have a student take a cut-out from the bag and read it aloud slowly two times.
4. Groups should work together to determine which item does not belong and why.
5. Choose a student to announce her group's answer. Other students should each show a thumbs-up if they agree.
6. After the student with the cut-out confirms the correct answer, set aside the cut-out and let another student choose a cut-out. The activity continues until all of the cut-outs have been used or all students have taken turns.
7. When the activity is complete, store the cut-outs in the bag.

Teacher Note: One answer has been given on each activity card. However, several answers may be possible. Check students' answers as needed.

What Does Not Belong?

1. Work in groups of 3–4 students.
2. One student should take a cut-out from the bag and read it aloud slowly two times.
3. Groups should work together to determine which item does not belong and why.
4. One student should announce her group's answer. Other students should each show a thumbs-up if they agree. The student with the cut-out should confirm the correct answer.
5. The student should set aside the cut-out and pass the bag to another student to take a turn. The activity continues until all of the cut-outs have been used or all students have taken turns.
6. When the activity is complete, store the cut-outs in the bag.

What Does Not Belong?

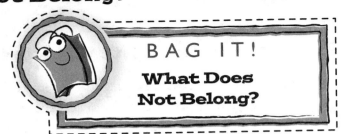

BAG IT!

What Does Not Belong?

▲			▲	
swings monkey bars slide desks	Desks are not found on a playground.	squirrel deer raccoon crocodile	A crocodile is not a forest animal.
lettuce pineapple green beans broccoli	A pineapple is not a vegetable.	eyes elbow nose mouth	An elbow is not a facial feature.
zebra giraffe whale lion	A whale is not a land animal.	earrings bracelet necklace pants	Pants are not jewelry.
cookies cake pie lemonade	Lemonade is not a dessert.	police officer firefighter hose truck	A police officer is not found in a firehouse.
car backpack truck train	A backpack is not a vehicle.	mayonnaise mustard ketchup bread	Bread is not a condiment (spread).
orange apple plum eggplant	An eggplant is not a fruit.	whale python octopus shark	A python is not an ocean animal.

What Does Not Belong?

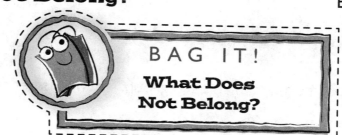

BAG IT!
What Does Not Belong?

plains oceans lakes rivers	Plains are not bodies of water.
egg tadpole fish frog	A fish is not a stage of frog life.
television newspaper book magazine	A television is not something to read.
mother neighbor brother sister	A neighbor is not a family member.
football baseball bat glove	A football is not used in baseball.
owl butterfly eagle hawk	A butterfly is not a bird.

scissors hammer knife saw	A hammer is not a cutting tool.
apple juice milk orange juice cereal	Cereal is not a drink.
skateboard car truck bicycle	A bicycle does not have four wheels.
duck fish swan goose	A fish is not a bird that can swim.
ruler pencil pen marker	A ruler is not a writing tool.
nail screw bolt hammer	A hammer is not a fastening device.

Name: _____ Date: _____

Circle the item that does not belong in each group. Then, answer the question.

1. sun   clouds   moon   ocean

    How is the item different? _____

2. spider   bee   snake   butterfly

    How is the item different? _____

3. sister   grandfather   brother   uncle

    How is the item different? _____

- - - ✂ -

Name: _____ Date: _____

Circle the item that does not belong in each group. Then, answer the question.

1. rooster   kitten   puppy   calf

    How is the item different? _____

2. cow   goat   chicken   sheep

    How is the item different? _____

3. lobster   shark   clam   crab

    How is the item different? _____

More Than One Meaning

Programming Instructions

Two levels of activity cards have been provided. In each level, students are required to listen to two definitions and think of the word that can have both meanings. The levels increase in difficulty from the Apprentice Level (page 22) to the Expert Level (page 23). Select an activity level. For a challenge, mix the levels together. Copy and cut apart the activity cards and attach each one to the front of a Colorful Cut-Out™. Decorate the front of a colorful gift bag with an extra cut-out from the set and attach the Bag It! Label (page 22 or 23). Copy and cut out the activity directions (below) and attach them to the back of the bag. Place the cut-outs inside the bag. Assess students' skill mastery using the Pretest and Posttest (page 24).

Objective

Students will listen to pairs of definitions and determine the homographs that are being defined.

Activity Directions

1. Divide the class into small groups of 3–4 students.
2. Shuffle the cut-outs and place them in the bag.
3. Have a student take a cut-out from the bag and read it aloud slowly two times.
4. Groups should work together to think of one word that can have both of the definitions.
5. Choose a student to announce his group's answer. Other students should each show a thumbs-up if they agree.
6. After the student with the cut-out confirms the correct answer, set aside the cut-out and let another student choose a cut-out. The activity continues until all of the cut-outs have been used or all students have taken turns.
7. When the activity is complete, store the cut-outs in the bag.

More Than One Meaning

1. Work in groups of 3–4 students.
2. One student should take a cut-out from the bag and read it aloud slowly two times.
3. Groups should work together to think of one word that can have both of the definitions.
4. One student should announce his group's answer. Other students should each show a thumbs-up if they agree. The student with the cut-out should confirm the correct answer.
5. The student should set aside the cut-out and pass the bag to another student to take a turn. The activity continues until all of the cut-outs have been used or all students have taken turns.
6. When the activity is complete, store the cut-outs in the bag.

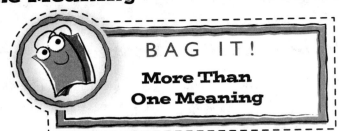

BAG IT!
More Than One Meaning

1. a small amount of time 2. after the first	**second**
1. a round object 2. a formal dance	**ball**
1. a flying animal 2. an object used in baseball	**bat**
1. a bird that quacks 2. to lower yourself suddenly	**duck**
1. a type of insect 2. to move through the air	**fly**
1. belonging to me 2. a place where coal is found	**mine**

1. a writing tool 2. an enclosed area for animals	**pen**
1. a baseball player 2. a container for pouring liquid	**pitcher**
1. a place for learning 2. a group of fish	**school**
1. opposite of right 2. past tense of leave	**left**
1. a gift 2. opposite of absent	**present**
1. a type of jewelry 2. the sound of a telephone	**ring**

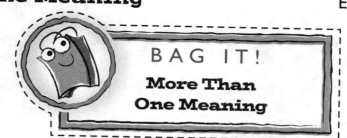

BAG IT!

More Than One Meaning

■ 1. to bend at the waist 2. the front part of a ship	bow	■ 1. a game played on a felt-covered table 2. a tank of water	pool
■ 1. a deep, round dish 2. to knock down pins with a ball	bowl	■ 1. a paddle used in tennis 2. a loud noise	racket
■ 1. a rooster's loud cry 2. a large, black bird	crow	■ 1. tools for weighing 2. the outer covering of a fish	scales
■ 1. to cut or trim 2. to fasten together	clip	■ 1. the inside of a hand 2. a type of tree	palm
■ 1. to shut 2. nearby	close	■ 1. the space around a house 2. a measurement that equals 36 inches	yard
■ 1. the underground part of a plant 2. to cheer	root	■ 1. a toy that spins 2. the highest point	top

Name: _____ Date: _____

More Than One Meaning Pretest

Read each pair of definitions. Write the word that has both meanings.

1. a cutting tool; the past tense of the word *see* _____

2. to press flat; a yellow vegetable _____

3. a small bird; to push something that is in the
   mouth through the throat and into the stomach _____

4. not heavy; not dark _____

- - - ✂ -

Name: _____ Date: _____

More Than One Meaning Posttest

Read each pair of definitions. Write the word that has both meanings.

1. the sound of a clock; a small insect _____

2. a brown spot on the skin;
   a small, underground animal _____

3. the past tense of the word *leave*;
   the direction that is the opposite of right _____

4. a deep hole dug to find water; in good health _____

Using Verb Tenses

Programming Instructions

Two levels of activity cards have been provided. The Apprentice Level (page 26) requires students to compose sentences using the present, past, and future tenses of regular verbs. The Expert Level (page 27) requires students to compose sentences using the present, past, and future tenses of irregular verbs. Select an activity level. For a challenge, mix the levels together. Copy and cut apart the activity cards and attach each one to the front of a Colorful Cut-Out™. Decorate the front of a colorful gift bag with an extra cut-out from the set and attach the Bag It! Label (page 26 or 27). Copy and cut out the activity directions (below) and attach them to the back of the bag. Place the cut-outs inside the bag. Assess students' skill mastery using the Pretest and Posttest (page 28).

Objective

Students will compose sentences using the present, past, and future tenses of regular and irregular verbs.

Activity Directions

1. Divide the class into small groups of 3–4 students. Give paper and pencils to each group.
2. Shuffle the cut-outs and place them in the bag.
3. Have a student take a cut-out from the bag and read it aloud slowly two times.
4. Groups should work together to write three sentences using the specified verb.
5. Choose a student to read her group's sentences aloud. Other students should each show a thumbs-up if they agree with the usage of the verb. Confirm appropriate sentences as needed.
6. Set aside the cut-out and let another student choose a cut-out. The activity continues until all of the cut-outs have been used or all students have taken turns. (Or, depending on how long it takes students to write all of the sentences, consider using only six cut-outs at a time.)
7. When the activity is complete, store the cut-outs in the bag.

Using Verb Tenses

1. Work in groups of 3–4 students. Each group needs paper and pencils.
2. One student should take a cut-out from the bag and read it aloud slowly two times.
3. Groups should work together to follow the directions and write three sentences.
4. One student should read her group's sentences aloud. Other students should each show a thumbs-up if they agree that the verb tenses were used correctly.
5. The student should set aside the cut-out and pass the bag to another student to take a turn. The activity continues until all of the cut-outs have been used or all students have taken turns.
6. When the activity is complete, store the cut-outs in the bag.

Name: _____ Date: _____

Follow the directions.

1. Write a sentence using the verb *bake* in the present tense.

    _____

2. Write a sentence using the verb *bake* in the past tense.

    _____

3. Write a sentence using the verb *bake* in the future tense.

    _____

✂ -

Name: _____ Date: _____

Using Verb Tenses Posttest

Follow the directions.

1. Write a sentence using the verb *take* in the present tense.

    _____

2. Write a sentence using the verb *take* in the past tense.

    _____

3. Write a sentence using the verb *take* in the future tense.

    _____

Solving Analogies

Programming Instructions

Two levels of activity cards have been provided. The Apprentice Level (page 30) requires students to solve analogies that focus on synonyms and antonyms. The Expert Level (page 31) requires students to solve analogies that focus on part/whole relationships and categories. Select an activity level. For a challenge, mix the levels together. Copy and cut apart the activity cards and attach each one to the front of a Colorful Cut-Out™. Decorate the front of a colorful gift bag with an extra cut-out from the set and attach the Bag It! Label (page 30 or 31). Copy and cut out the activity directions (below) and attach them to the back of the bag. Place the cut-outs inside the bag. Assess students' skill mastery using the Pretest and Posttest (page 32).

Objective

Students will solve analogies.

Activity Directions

1. Divide the class into small groups of 3–4 students.
2. Shuffle the cut-outs and place them in the bag.
3. Have a student take a cut-out from the bag and read it aloud slowly two times. Write the analogy on the board or a piece of chart paper.
4. Groups should work together to solve the analogy.
5. Choose a student to announce his group's answer. Other students should each show a thumbs-up if they agree. The student who is holding the cut-out should confirm the correct answer. Confirm appropriate alternative answers as needed.
6. Set aside the cut-out and let another student choose a cut-out. The activity continues until all of the cut-outs have been used or all students have taken turns.
7. When the activity is complete, store the cut-outs in the bag.

Teacher Note: If needed, remind students how to read an analogy before the activity begins. For example, *calf : cow :: piglet : _____* would be read *Calf is to cow as piglet is to _____ .*

Solving Analogies

1. Work in groups of 3–4 students.
2. One student should take a cut-out from the bag and read it aloud slowly two times. A teacher should write the analogy on the board or a piece of chart paper.
3. Groups should work together to solve the analogy.
4. One student should announce his group's answer. Other students should each show a thumbs-up if they agree. The student who is holding the cut-out should confirm the correct answer.
5. The student should set aside the cut-out and pass the bag to another student to take a turn. The activity continues until all of the cut-outs have been used or all students have taken turns.
6. When the activity is complete, store the cut-outs in the bag.

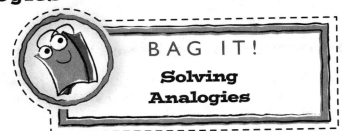

BAG IT!
Solving Analogies

▲ on : off ::
top : _____

bottom

▲ driver : bus ::
pilot : _____

airplane

▲ heavy : light ::
loud : _____

quiet

▲ win : lose ::
start : _____

stop

▲ smooth : rough ::
old : _____

young

▲ strong : weak ::
polite : _____

rude

▲ listen : hear ::
look : _____

view

▲ princess : prince ::
queen : _____

king

▲ finger : hand ::
toe : _____

foot

▲ warm : hot ::
cool : _____

cold

▲ teacher : class ::
coach : _____

team

▲ kitten : cat ::
puppy : _____

dog

Solving Analogies

BAG IT!
Solving Analogies

---

possess : own ::
discover : _____

find

timid : shy ::
cautious : _____

careful

---

letter : word ::
sentence : _____

paragraph

friend : enemy ::
teammate : _____

opponent

---

pitcher : baseball ::
quarterback : _____

(American) football

prevent : stop ::
view : _____

look

---

frog : amphibian ::
tiger : _____

mammal

pig : snout ::
elephant : _____

trunk

---

mouse : mice ::
goose : _____

geese

bird : feathers ::
fish : _____

scales

---

scale : weight ::
thermometer : _____

temperature

child : children ::
ox : _____

oxen

Solving Analogies Pretest

Solve the analogies.

1. wife : husband :: aunt : _____

2. stop : go :: sad : _____

3. asleep : awake :: laughing : _____

4. ink : pen :: paint : _____

- - ✂ -

Solving Analogies Posttest

Solve the analogies.

1. close : open :: remember : _____

2. work : play :: scream : _____

3. bear : mammal :: snake : _____

4. ladder : firefighter :: hammer : _____

Programming Instructions

Make a copy of the Math Marathon Story (pages 34–36) for each group. Make a copy of the Math Marathon Answer Key (pages 37–39) for each group or make a copy on a transparency for an overhead projector. This activity requires students to work together to read a story and edit for conventions. Copy and cut apart the activity cards and attach each one to the front of a Colorful Cut-Out™. Decorate the front of a colorful gift bag with an extra cut-out from the set and attach the Bag It! Label (page 40). Copy and cut out the activity directions (below) and attach them to the back of the bag. Place the cut-outs inside the bag. Assess students' skill mastery using the Pretest and Posttest (page 41).

Objective

Students will read a story and edit for conventions.

Activity Directions

1. Divide students into five small groups. Give each group a copy of the story and colorful pencils or pens.
2. Shuffle the programmed cut-outs and place them in the bag.
3. Have groups read the story together. (If desired, read the story aloud and have groups follow on their copies.)
4. Have one student from each group take a cut-out from the bag.
5. Groups should read their cut-outs to determine which section of the story they will be editing and how many errors they will be looking for. (If desired, provide a list of the types of errors they should find—commas, periods, exclamation points, question marks, quotation marks, apostrophes, spelling, subject-verb agreement, and capitalization.)
6. Each group should work together to edit their section of the story using colorful pencils or pens.
7. When all groups are finished editing, show the answer key transparency or give each group a copy of the answer key to check their work. Have each group present their answers as classmates follow on the answer key or the transparency. (In some cases, students may use periods and exclamation points interchangeably. Confirm appropriate variations as needed.)
8. When the activity is complete, store the cut-outs in the bag.

Teacher Note: If time allows, let each group edit the entire story for extra practice.

Editing for Conventions

1. Work in five small groups. Each group needs a copy of the story and colorful pencils or pens.
2. Groups should read the story together.
3. One student from each group should take a cut-out from the bag.
4. Each group should read their cut-out to determine which section of the story to edit and how many errors to look for.
5. Each group should work together to edit their section of the story using colorful pencils or pens.
6. When all groups are finished editing, they should use the answer key to check their work. Or, each group can present their answers to the other groups.
7. When the activity is complete, store the cut-outs in the bag.

Math Marathon

◆   Last week, our class decided to challenge the other third-grade classes to a math marathon We think were the best with multiplication facts, and we beleive we can answer any place value or measurement question faster than any other class.

We plans too hold the event next Saturday morning in the cafeteria. Our teacher, Miss Jackson, asked the principal "Will you encurage the other classes to participate" The principal agreed to help

We spent Monday morning making invitations. It was hard to keep our plan a secret. On Tuesday, jacko's pizza offered to throw a pizza party for the winning class. We all yelled, Hooray That should have every third graders mouth watering.

★   The other classes have until Friday to acept our challenge. Miss Jackson asked to third-grade math teachers from smith elementary school to prepare the questions.

Friday has finally arrived, and every class has accepted our challenge We has so much work to do before next Saturday

On the playground, every third grader talk about being the winner.
Its not going to be easy to win the marathon. Miss Jackson said I
am proud of you becuz you created sumthing new and exciting at
our school.

✖   It is finally Saturday morning, and our class is waiting at the cafeteria
door to greet guests and make sure everything is ready. Before we
begin, the principal tell every body the rules. The assistant principal
Mrs. Jessup will read the questions, and the school librarian will be the
timekeeper. Hour principle, Mr. carter, ends by saying, "I wish all of the
third graders good luck! I am proud of all of you for working so hard.
This event is already a huge success Now, let the math marathon begin"

The two team captains for each class have their classmates sitting
around them. The first question go to our class. How many sides does
an octagon have One of our captains responds, "eight!" We earn one
point. Everyone claps, and a question goes to the next class. At the
end of the first round, the score are tied. Every class answered their
question correctly.

✔ When we take a break to relax the score is tied at five for each class. The excitment is high After a few minutes, Mrs. Jessup takes the microphone. She is ready to ask us our sixth question. "how many inches are in one yard

Alex responds, There are 36 inches in one yard" Our class have a score of six points. Later, one class makes a mistake, and our class gets the bonus point. Another class miss the time limit. Now, two classes are tied for first place. every other class is only won point away. The questions get harder. At the end of round 10 three classes are tied for first place. Wow, what a saturday this has turned out to be

❀ After sum of the tie-breaker questions, the score are still tied with only two more questions One little mistake will give one class a chance to move ahead.

Mr. Carter takes the microphone and says, Ive just talked to Mrs. Alvarez the PTA President and the pta wishes to make every third-grade class a winner in this close contest. The pizza restarant will throw a great pizza party for all of the students. Congratulations, third graders The cafeteria fills with claping cheering, and excitement!

Math Marathon Answer Key

◆ Last week, our class decided to challenge the other third-grade classes to a math marathon. We think we're the best with multiplication facts, and we believe we can answer any place value or measurement question faster than any other class.

We plans too hold the event next Saturday morning in the cafeteria. Our teacher, Miss Jackson, asked the principal, "Will you encourage the other classes to participate?" The principal agreed to help.

We spent Monday morning making invitations. It was hard to keep our plan a secret. On Tuesday, jacko's pizza offered to throw a pizza party for the winning class. We all yelled, "Hooray! That should have every third graders mouth watering.

★ The other classes have until Friday to accept our challenge. Miss Jackson asked to third-grade math teachers from smith elementary school to prepare the questions.

Friday has finally arrived, and every class has accepted our challenge. We has so much work to do before next Saturday.

On the playground, every third grader talk*s* about being the winner. It's not going to be easy to win the marathon. Miss Jackson said*,* "I am proud of you*,* ~~becuz~~ *because* you created ~~sumthing~~ *something* new and exciting at our school."

✖ It is finally Saturday morning, and our class is waiting at the cafeteria door to greet guests and make sure everything is ready. Before we begin, the principal tell*s* every*body* the rules. The assistant principal*,* Mrs. Jessup*,* will read the questions, and the school librarian will be the timekeeper. *p*our principl*e,* Mr. *c*arter, ends by saying, "I wish all of the third graders good luck! I am proud of all of you for working so hard. This event is already a huge success*.* Now, let the math marathon begin*!*"

The two team captains for each class have their classmates sitting around them. The first question go*es* to our class. "How many sides does an octagon have*?*" One of our captains responds, "*e*ight!" We earn one point. Everyone claps, and a question goes to the next class. At the end of the first round, the score *is* ~~are~~ tied. Every class answered their question correctly.

✔ When we take a break to relax, the score is tied at five for each class. The excitment is high. After a few minutes, Mrs. Jessup takes the microphone. She is ready to ask us our sixth question. "how many inches are in one yard?"

Alex responds, "There are 36 inches in one yard." Our class have a score of six points. Later, one class makes a mistake, and our class gets the bonus point. Another class miss the time limit. Now, two classes are tied for first place. every other class is only won point away. The questions get harder. At the end of round 10, three classes are tied for first place. Wow, what a saturday this has turned out to be!

❁ After sum of the tie-breaker questions, the score are still tied with only two more questions. One little mistake will give one class a chance to move ahead.

Mr. Carter takes the microphone and says, "Ive just talked to Mrs. Alvarez, the PTA President and the pta wishes to make every third-grade class a winner in this close contest. The pizza restarant will throw a great pizza party for all of the students. Congratulations, third graders. The cafeteria fills with claping, cheering, and excitement!

BAG IT!
Editing for Conventions

◆ Work together to edit the section of the story that has a ◆.
There are 15 errors.

★ Work together to edit the section of the story that has a ★.
There are 15 errors.

✖ Work together to edit the section of the story that has a ✖.
There are 15 errors.

✔ Work together to edit the section of the story that has a ✔.
There are 15 errors.

✿ Work together to edit the section of the story that has a ✿.
There are 15 errors.

Name: _____ Date: _____

Edit each sentence. Then, write each sentence correctly.

1. the math marathon will be a fantastik event for everyone

    _____

2. do you think the compitition will start on time asked Margaret.

    _____

3. Wow Our class did a great job planing setting up, and hosting

    _____

- - - ✂ -

Name: _____ Date: _____

Editing for Conventions Posttest

Edit each sentence. Then, write each sentence correctly.

1. I cant believe the math marathon was so close exclamed Marcus.

    _____

2. "I know," said Victoria Do you thinks everyone had fun

    _____

3. it seemed like everone had a fabulous time said miss jackson

    _____

Programming Instructions

Two levels of activity cards have been provided. The Apprentice Level (page 43) requires students to listen to sentences, determine whether they are complete or incomplete, and suggest corrections for incomplete sentences. The Expert Level (page 44) requires students to listen to sentences, determine whether they are complete or run-ons, and suggest corrections for run-on sentences. Select an activity level. For a challenge, mix the levels together. Copy and cut apart the activity cards and attach each one to the back of a Colorful Cut-Out™. You will also need five cut-outs without activity cards on them. Assess students' skill mastery using the Pretest and Posttest (page 45).

Objectives

Students will listen to sentences and determine if they are complete, incomplete, or run-ons. Students will suggest corrections for incomplete and run-on sentences.

Activity Directions

1. Choose five programmed cut-outs and shuffle them with the five blank cut-outs.
2. Have 10 students sit in a circle on the floor.
3. Give each student a cut-out with the activity card facedown. (The text should not be visible.) Instruct students not to look at the backs of the cut-outs.
4. Give a signal for students to start quickly passing the cut-outs around the circle. Each student should be holding only one cut-out at a time.
5. At the next signal, students should stop passing the cut-outs and look at the backs of the cut-outs they are holding.
6. Students with programmed cut-outs should raise their hands.
7. Have one of these students read the sentence aloud slowly two times. (If desired, write the sentence on the board or a piece of chart paper.)
8. Have each student take a moment to think about the sentence.
9. At your signal, students should each show a thumbs-up if they believe the sentence is complete, a scissor-cutting motion if they believe the sentence is incomplete, or a hand-over-hand rolling motion if they believe the sentence is a run-on. The student holding the cut-out should confirm the correct answer. Select one or two students to offer suggestions for correcting incomplete and run-on sentences.
10. Set aside the cut-out and let another student take a turn.
11. When the five programmed cut-outs have been used, prepare the circle for another round by shuffling the five blank cut-outs with five more programmed cut-outs. The activity continues until all of the cut-outs have been used or all students have taken turns.
12. When the activity is complete, store the cut-outs in a resealable plastic bag or a labeled envelope.

We have been studying and working hard in third grade this year.

complete

Jarrod watches movies every Saturday night with.

incomplete

Casey likes to eat spinach with his dinner, but Aaron will not touch it.

complete

To read 100 books before she finishes third grade.

incomplete

Mia rides the bus with her mom after school every day.

complete

Thomas runs so much faster than.

incomplete

Mr. and Mrs. Palmer crossed the street and went inside the grocery store.

complete

Many third graders are eight years old, but some.

incomplete

Katie likes to do science experiments and has learned many interesting things.

complete

During recess, our whole class enjoys.

incomplete

Our local firefighters practice fire drills every Friday afternoon outside the station.	complete	We go to the gym and they go to music and we all go to art on Thursdays.	run-on
Gabe's family went on vacation to Asia, where they toured the Great Wall of China.	complete	Sierra told everyone about her fabulous trip to the beach Trey was very jealous.	run-on
Every day, Tisha goes home from school, eats a snack, and rides her bike.	complete	We asked many complicated questions they told us all of the answers that we needed to know.	run-on
Cole and Joshua spent hours sliding down the big hill on their sleds.	complete	Karen loves writing with her sparkling purple pen Nikki writes with a shiny pink pen.	run-on
I went to the market with my cousin to buy pears, apples, beans, and potatoes.	complete	The other third-grade class is learning about our state we are learning about the election process.	run-on

Sentence Roundup Pretest

Read each sentence. Circle the type of sentence that it is.

1. Friday is my favorite day of the week because it starts the weekend.
   a. complete
   b. incomplete
   c. run-on

2. John went to the gym Rachel went to to lunch Tara read a book.
   a. complete
   b. incomplete
   c. run-on

3. Yesterday, after our class returned from the library.
   a. complete
   b. incomplete
   c. run-on

- - - ✂ -

Sentence Roundup Posttest

Read each sentence. Circle the type of sentence that it is.

1. Watched movies, ate popcorn, and played computer games.
   a. complete
   b. incomplete
   c. run-on

2. Our class won the award for reading the most books in one month.
   a. complete
   b. incomplete
   c. run-on

3. Our teacher helps us practice multiplication tables we are improving.
   a. complete
   b. incomplete
   c. run-on

Programming Instructions

Three levels of activity cards have been provided. The Novice Level (page 47) requires students to count the number of syllables in one- and two-syllable words. The Apprentice Level (page 48) requires students to count the number of syllables in two- and three-syllable words. The Expert Level (page 49) requires students to count the number of syllables in three- and four-syllable words. Select an activity level. For a challenge, mix the levels together. Copy and cut apart the activity cards and attach each one to the back of a Colorful Cut-Out™. You will also need six cut-outs without activity cards on them. Assess students' skill mastery using the Pretest and Posttest (page 50).

Objective

Students will count the number of syllables in one-, two-, three-, and four-syllable words.

Activity Directions

1. Choose six programmed cut-outs and shuffle them with the six blank cut-outs.
2. Have 12 students sit in a circle on the floor.
3. Give each student a cut-out with the activity card facedown. (The text should not be visible.) Instruct students not to look at the backs of the cut-outs.
4. Give a signal for students to start quickly passing the cut-outs around the circle. Each student should be holding only one cut-out at a time.
5. At the next signal, students should stop passing the cut-outs and look at the backs of the cut-outs they are holding.
6. Students with programmed cut-outs should raise their hands.
7. Have one of these students read the word aloud slowly two times. Write the word on the board or a piece of chart paper.
8. Have each student take a moment to think about the syllables in the word.
9. Have students say the word aloud slowly and then count the syllables aloud. (If desired, select a student to draw lines on the board or piece of chart paper to separate the syllables.) The student holding the cut-out should confirm the correct answer.
10. Set aside the cut-out and let another student take a turn.
11. When the six programmed cut-outs have been used, prepare the circle for another round by shuffling the six blank cut-outs with six more programmed cut-outs. The activity continues until all of the cut-outs have been used or all students have taken turns.
12. When the activity is complete, store the cut-outs in a resealable plastic bag or a labeled envelope.

Teacher Note: If desired, point to the syllables on the board or piece of chart paper as students count aloud.

books	1 syllable	table	2 syllables; ta•ble
swings	1 syllable	window	2 syllables; win•dow
desk	1 syllable	teacher	2 syllables; tea•cher
chair	1 syllable	pencil	2 syllables; pen•cil
lunch	1 syllable	backpack	2 syllables; back•pack
clock	1 syllable	playground	2 syllables; play•ground

▲ ruler	2 syllables; ru•ler	▲ eraser	3 syllables; e•ra•ser
▲ student	2 syllables; stu•dent	▲ projector	3 syllables; pro•jec•tor
▲ crayons	2 syllables; cray•ons	▲ vacation	3 syllables; va•ca•tion
▲ stapler	2 syllables; sta•pler	▲ computer	3 syllables; com•pu•ter
▲ study	2 syllables; stu•dy	▲ subtraction	3 syllables; sub•trac•tion
▲ divide	2 syllables; di•vide	▲ multiply	3 syllables; mul•ti•ply

principal	3 syllables; prin•ci•pal	television	4 syllables; te•le•vi•sion
monitor	3 syllables; mo•ni•tor	librarian	4 syllables; li•brar•i•an
sharpener	3 syllables; shar•pe•ner	secretary	4 syllables; se•cre•tar•y
library	3 syllables; li•brar•y	dictionary	4 syllables; dic•tio•nar•y
calendar	3 syllables; ca•len•dar	calculator	4 syllables; cal•cu•la•tor
addition	3 syllables; a•ddi•tion	thermometer	4 syllables; ther•mo•me•ter

Name: _____ Date: _____

Counting Syllables Pretest

Read each word to yourself. Circle the number of syllables in each word.

1. Monday
   a. one
   b. two
   c. three
   d. four

2. desks
   a. one
   b. two
   c. three
   d. four

3. locker
   a. one
   b. two
   c. three
   d. four

4. synonym
   a. one
   b. two
   c. three
   d. four

5. classroom
   a. one
   b. two
   c. three
   d. four

6. gymnasium
   a. one
   b. two
   c. three
   d. four

-- --✁-- -- -- -- -- -- -- -- -- -- -- -- -- -- -- -- -- -- -- --

Name: _____ Date: _____

Counting Syllables Posttest

Read each word to yourself. Circle the number of syllables in each word.

1. understanding
   a. one
   b. two
   c. three
   d. four

2. thesaurus
   a. one
   b. two
   c. three
   d. four

3. textbooks
   a. one
   b. two
   c. three
   d. four

4. science
   a. one
   b. two
   c. three
   d. four

5. homophone
   a. one
   b. two
   c. three
   d. four

6. calculator
   a. one
   b. two
   c. three
   d. four

How Do You Spell the Plural?

Programming Instructions

Two levels of activity cards have been provided. The Apprentice Level (page 52) requires students to listen to the singular forms of nouns and spell the plurals using -s and -es endings. The Expert Level (page 53) requires students to listen to the singular forms of nouns and spell the plurals using -ies and -ves endings, as well as irregular spellings. Select an activity level. For a challenge, mix the levels together. Copy and cut apart the activity cards and attach each one to the back of a Colorful Cut-Out™. You will also need six cut-outs without activity cards on them. Assess students' skill mastery using the Pretest and Posttest (page 54).

Objective

Students will spell the plural forms of nouns.

Activity Directions

1. Choose six programmed cut-outs and shuffle them with the six blank cut-outs.
2. Have 12 students sit in a circle on the floor.
3. Give each student a cut-out with the activity card facedown. (The text should not be visible.) Instruct students not to look at the backs of the cut-outs.
4. Give a signal for students to start quickly passing the cut-outs around the circle. Each student should be holding only one cut-out at a time.
5. At the next signal, students should stop passing the cut-outs and look at the backs of the cut-outs they are holding.
6. Students with programmed cut-outs should raise their hands.
7. Have one of these students read the word aloud slowly two times. If necessary, the student can spell the singular form of the word aloud. Also, the word can be written on the board or a piece of chart paper.
8. Have each student take a moment to think about how to spell the plural form of the word and whisper her answer to a neighbor.
9. The student holding the cut-out should choose a classmate to answer aloud. Other students should each show a thumbs-up if they agree. The student holding the cut-out should confirm the correct answer.
10. Set aside the cut-out and let another student take a turn.
11. When the six programmed cut-outs have been used, prepare the circle for another round by shuffling the six blank cut-outs with six more programmed cut-outs. The activity continues until all of the cut-outs have been used or all students have taken turns.
12. When the activity is complete, store the cut-outs in a resealable plastic bag or a labeled envelope.

Teacher Note: If desired, provide paper and pencils and have students write each word during step 8.

dancer	dancers	story	stories
family	families	box	boxes
key	keys	glass	glasses
elephant	elephants	fox	foxes
candy	candies	boss	bosses
deer	deer	moose	moose

gulf	gulfs	tomato	tomatoes
taxi	taxis	leaf	leaves
wife	wives	thief	thieves
half	halves	man	men
radio	radios	tooth	teeth
zero	zeroes	goose	geese

▲ Paul was <u>sad</u> when his last baseball game was cancelled.

gloomy, miserable, sorrowful

▲ The skyscrapers downtown are <u>big</u>.

huge, gigantic, enormous

▲ The <u>pretty</u> flower is the most popular exhibit at the garden.

stunning, exquisite, elegant

▲ Pam is <u>happy</u> about her new kitten.

glad, thrilled, delighted

▲ Mrs. Henderson makes <u>good</u> cookies for us.

scrumptious, marvelous, delightful

▲ Jan thought of a <u>smart</u> plan for winning the science fair.

brilliant, (an) intelligent, clever

▲ The <u>little</u> ballerina floated across the stage like a feather.

tiny, petite, pint-sized

▲ Nick struggled to build the toy because the directions were <u>hard</u>.

confusing, difficult, complicated

▲ Mr. Phipps is <u>nice</u> when we go to his house for piano lessons.

courteous, gracious, kind

▲ Nancy was <u>tired</u> after a sleepless night.

exhausted, drained, weary

▲ My favorite cartoon character is <u>funny</u>.

amusing, hilarious, comical

▲ The <u>mean</u> lion was roaring all day!

unfriendly, ferocious, vicious

Jack <u>said</u>, "There is a terrible storm coming!"

exclaimed, shouted, proclaimed

My family is <u>going</u> to Australia on vacation!

traveling, escaping, journeying

The children <u>laughed</u> at the movie they were watching.

giggled, howled, chuckled

Sean's mom <u>looked at</u> the broken glass on the kitchen floor.

examined, inspected, analyzed

The rabbit <u>ran</u> across the field to escape from the fox.

dashed, scampered, sprinted

Hector <u>ate</u> a whole pizza after taking a three-hour hike.

devoured, consumed, savored

The man <u>walked</u> in the park on a lazy Sunday afternoon.

sauntered, strolled, meandered

Molly <u>asked</u> her brother about her missing doll.

questioned, quizzed, interrogated

Sara <u>saw</u> a beautiful butterfly sitting on a flower in the garden.

glimpsed, spied, noticed

Myla often <u>thinks about</u> the plot of her favorite chapter book.

examines, analyzes, considers

I <u>like</u> spending time with my grandparents.

treasure, cherish, enjoy

The majestic eagle <u>flies</u> through the sky.

soars, floats, glides

Name: _____ Date: _____

Read each sentence. Fill in the blank with a better word to replace the underlined word.

1. We ate a <u>good</u> dinner at my favorite restaurant.

    _____

2. Daniel is so <u>scared</u> of spiders that he will not walk in the woods.

    _____

3. The frog <u>jumped</u> over two turtles as it moved swiftly toward the pond.

    _____

- - - ✁ -

Name: _____ Date: _____

Focus on Word Choice Posttest

Read each sentence. Fill in the blank with a better word to replace the underlined word.

1. Craig was <u>hungry</u> after helping his dad rake the leaves.

    _____

2. Marisa <u>took</u> a cookie off the plate before her mom could stop her.

    _____

3. If we do not <u>go</u>, we will miss our plane!

    _____

Be an Expert: Alphabetical Order

Programming Instructions

Three levels of activity cards have been provided. The Novice Level (page 60) requires students to look at the first and second letters of words on cut-outs they are holding and stand in alphabetic order. The Apprentice Level (page 61) requires students to look at the second and third letters of words on cut-outs they are holding and stand in alphabetic order. The Expert Level (page 62) requires students to look at the third and fourth letters of words on cut-outs they are holding and stand in alphabetic order. Select an activity level. For a challenge, mix the levels together. Copy and cut apart the activity cards and attach each one to the front of a Colorful Cut-Out™. Decorate the front of a file folder with an extra cut-out from the set and label the folder with the title of the activity. Staple a large, resealable plastic bag inside the file folder. Place the cut-outs inside the bag. Assess students' skill mastery using the Pretest and Posttest (page 63).

Objective

Students will stand in lines to alphabetize the words on cut-outs they are holding. Students will look at the first, second, third, and fourth letters of the words to alphabetize them.

Activity Directions

1. Shuffle the programmed cut-outs and place them in a pile.
2. Have a student take a cut-out, stand in front of the group, and read the word aloud.
3. Have another student take a cut-out, read the word aloud, and position herself in alphabetical order with the first student. Other students should each show a thumbs-up if they agree with the order. Confirm the order as needed.
4. The activity continues until all of the cut-outs have been used or all students have taken turns.
5. When the activity is complete, store the cut-outs in the bag inside the file folder.

Teacher Note: The correct order for the novice level is: raccoon, recess, rhinoceros, riddle, rodeo, rumble, sandwich, scarecrow, season, shadow, skunk, spaghetti.

The correct order for the apprentice level is: tablecloth, taste, teacher, telescope, theater, thirsty, ticket, tired, today, tooth, traffic, triangle.

The correct order for the expert level is: pace, packing, paddle, padlock, pail, painter, panda, panic, parallel, parent, pathway, pattern.

raccoon

recess

rhinoceros

riddle

rodeo

rumble

sandwich

scarecrow

season

shadow

skunk

spaghetti

60

tablecloth

taste

teacher

telescope

theater

thirsty

ticket

tired

today

tooth

traffic

triangle

pace	packing
paddle	padlock
pail	painter
panda	panic
parallel	parent
pathway	pattern

Name: _____ Date: _____

Read each set of words. Write them in alphabetical order.

1. mouth, lemon, monkey

   _____

2. dust, duck, door

   _____

3. victory, violin, vicious

   _____

- - ✂ -

Name: _____ Date: _____

Be an Expert: Alphabetical Order Posttest

Read each set of words. Write them in alphabetical order.

1. barnyard, cheesecake, basket

   _____

2. firewood, ferret, feather

   _____

3. elephant, elevator, element

   _____

Be an Expert: It's a Noun and a Verb

Programming Instructions

This activity requires each student to listen to two statements and stand in the line that corresponds to the statement with which he agrees or stand in a third line if he agrees with both statements. Copy and cut apart the activity cards and attach each one to the front of a Colorful Cut-Out™. Decorate the front of a file folder with an extra cut-out from the set and label the folder with the title of the activity. Staple a large, resealable plastic bag inside the file folder. Place the cut-outs inside the bag. Assess students' skill mastery using the Pretest and Posttest (page 67).

Objectives

Students will make living bar graphs by standing in lines that correspond to statements with which they agree. Students will compose sentences using words that can be both nouns and verbs.

Activity Directions

1. Shuffle the programmed cut-outs and place them in a pile.
2. Have a student take a cut-out and give it to you.
3. Read the statements on the cut-out aloud to the whole group.
4. Each student should take a moment to decide which statement he agrees with. (Some students may not agree with either of the statements on the cut-out, and some students may agree with both statements.)
5. Read the statements aloud again. Pause between the statements and indicate where students should line up for each statement. (Students should form three lines—one for agreement with the first statement, one for agreement with the second statement, and one for agreement with both statements.)
6. After the lines are formed, select a few students from each line to share their sentences aloud. Other students should each show a thumbs-up if they agree with the usage of the words. Confirm answers as needed.
7. Have students return to their seats.
8. Set aside the cut-out and let another student take a turn. The activity continues until all of the cut-outs have been used or all students have taken turns. (All students will not participate in every lineup, but the statements are designed so that each student should be a part of several lineups.)
9. When the activity is complete, store the cut-outs in the bag inside the file folder.

Line up if you can make a sentence using *tip* as a noun.
Line up if you can make a sentence using *tip* as a verb.

Line up if you can make a sentence using *duck* as a noun.
Line up if you can make a sentence using *duck* as a verb.

Line up if you can make a sentence using *break* as a noun.
Line up if you can make a sentence using *break* as a verb.

Line up if you can make a sentence using *light* as a noun.
Line up if you can make a sentence using *light* as a verb.

Line up if you can make a sentence using *check* as a noun.
Line up if you can make a sentence using *check* as a verb.

Line up if you can make a sentence using *buckle* as a noun.
Line up if you can make a sentence using *buckle* as a verb.

Line up if you can make a sentence using *fall* as a noun.
Line up if you can make a sentence using *fall* as a verb.

Line up if you can make a sentence using *play* as a noun.
Line up if you can make a sentence using *play* as a verb.

Line up if you can make a sentence using *change* as a noun.
Line up if you can make a sentence using *change* as a verb.

Line up if you can make a sentence using *water* as a noun.
Line up if you can make a sentence using *water* as a verb.

Line up if you can make a sentence using *fly* as a noun.
Line up if you can make a sentence using *fly* as a verb.

Line up if you can make a sentence using *puzzle* as a noun.
Line up if you can make a sentence using *puzzle* as a verb.

Line up if you can make a sentence using *plant* as a noun.
Line up if you can make a sentence using *plant* as a verb.

Line up if you can make a sentence using *back* as a noun.
Line up if you can make a sentence using *back* as a verb.

Line up if you can make a sentence using *saw* as a noun.
Line up if you can make a sentence using *saw* as a verb.

Line up if you can make a sentence using *stick* as a noun.
Line up if you can make a sentence using *stick* as a verb.

Line up if you can make a sentence using *cook* as a noun.
Line up if you can make a sentence using *cook* as a verb.

Line up if you can make a sentence using *tire* as a noun.
Line up if you can make a sentence using *tire* as a verb.

Line up if you can make a sentence using *ski* as a noun.
Line up if you can make a sentence using *ski* as a verb.

Line up if you can make a sentence using *watch* as a noun.
Line up if you can make a sentence using *watch* as a verb.

Line up if you can make a sentence using *head* as a noun.
Line up if you can make a sentence using *head* as a verb.

Line up if you can make a sentence using *host* as a noun.
Line up if you can make a sentence using *host* as a verb.

Line up if you can make a sentence using *dash* as a noun.
Line up if you can make a sentence using *dash* as a verb.

Line up if you can make a sentence using *crowd* as a noun.
Line up if you can make a sentence using *crowd* as a verb.

Name: _____ Date: _____

Write a sentence using each word as a noun and a sentence using each word as a verb.

1. star

_____

_____

2. tag

_____

_____

- - - ✂ -

Name: _____ Date: _____

Be an Expert: It's a Noun and a Verb Posttest

Write a sentence using each word as a noun and a sentence using each word as a verb.

1. fire

_____

_____

2. sink

_____

_____

Using Your Senses

Programming Instructions

Make an enlarged copy of the Senses Chart (page 72) and display it on a wall or bulletin board. This activity requires students to examine everyday objects and describe them according to certain attributes. Collect a variety of common items, such as a short pencil, a marker, a broken crayon, a rock, a balloon, keys, aluminum foil, plastic wrap, sandpaper, cotton balls, or uncooked pasta, and put them in a box. Copy and cut apart the activity cards and attach each one to the front of a Colorful Cut-Out™. Decorate the front of a colorful gift bag with an extra cut-out from the set and attach the Attributes Label (below). Copy and cut out the activity directions (below) and attach them to the back of the bag. Place the cut-outs inside the bag.

Objectives

Students will examine various attributes of common items and describe certain aspects of each item in detail.

Activity Directions

1. Divide the class into small groups of 3–4 students.
2. Shuffle the programmed cut-outs and place them in the bag.
3. One student from each group should take a cut-out from the bag while another group member takes an item from the box.
4. Each student who selected a cut-out should read it aloud to his group.
5. Groups should work together to describe their items using the attributes on the cut-outs. (If desired, provide paper and pencils for students to record their descriptions.) Encourage students to use the senses chart as a reference if needed.
6. When all of the groups have completed their descriptions, one student from each group should present their description to the class.
7. Have students set aside the cut-outs and return their items to the box.
8. Let groups select new cut-outs and new items. The activity continues as time allows.
9. When the activity is complete, store the cut-outs in the bag.

A T T R I B U T E S

Using Your Senses

Using Your Senses

1. Work in groups of 3–4 students.
2. One student from each group should take a cut-out from the bag while another group member takes an item from the box.
3. Students should read the cut-outs aloud to their groups.
4. Each group should work together to describe their item using the directions on the cut-out.
5. One student from each group should present their description to the class.
6. The students should set aside the cut-outs and return the items to the box.
7. Each group should select a new cut-out and a new item. The activity continues as time allows.
8. When the activity is complete, store the cut-outs in the bag.

Shape

the way something looks; the outer form of something

Ask yourself: Is it round, rectangular, pointy, irregular, etc.?

Size

how big or small something is

Ask yourself: Is it bigger than a penny, smaller than an apple, about the same size as a dictionary, etc.?

Texture

the way something feels; the surface quality of something

Ask yourself: Is it rough, smooth, spongy, hard, soft, etc.?

Weight

how heavy something is; how much something weighs

Ask yourself: Is it heavier than a full backpack, lighter than a cat, about the same weight as a box of cereal, etc.?

Color

the hue of something

Ask yourself: Is it orange, red, yellowish, brownish-green, dark blue, light pink, etc.?

Function

the way something is used; the purpose of something

Ask yourself: How is it used? What is its purpose? What benefit does it provide?

Describe the shape.	Describe the shape.
Describe the size.	Describe the size.
Describe the texture.	Describe the texture.
Describe the weight.	Describe the weight.
Describe the color.	Describe the color.
Describe the function.	Describe the function.

Programming Instructions

This activity is designed for 12 students and requires them to fill in blanks in sentences using words and phrases that tell *who*, *what*, *when*, *where*, *why*, and *how*. Copy and cut apart the Cube Labels (page 75) and the activity cards. Attach each cube label and each activity card to the front of a Colorful Cut-Out™. Attach the cube label cut-outs to the sides of a large, inflatable cube. Or, make a cube using the directions on page 8. Assess students' skill mastery using the Pretest and Posttest (page 77).

Teacher Tip: Laminate the cut-outs and attach them to the cube with removable tape or hook-and-loop tape so that you can store them while using the cube for other activities.

Objective

Students will determine what is missing and complete partial sentences by filling in blanks using words and phrases that tell *who*, *what*, *when*, *where*, *why*, and *how*.

Activity Directions

1. Have 12 students sit on the floor in a circle.
2. Give each student a cut-out. Students should check the sentences on their cut-outs to determine what kind of word or phrase is missing—a *who*, *what*, *when*, *where*, *why*, or *how*.
3. Roll the cube for students.
4. Any student who has a sentence that is missing the type of word or phrase that is showing on the cube should raise her hand.
5. Choose one student and have her read her sentence aloud, first as written and then filling in the blank.
6. Other students should each show a thumbs-up if they agree that her sentence was missing the type of word or phrase that is showing on the cube and that she correctly filled in the blank.
7. Any student who can build on the answer using more descriptive words should raise his hand.
8. Choose 1–2 students to give their more descriptive answers. (For example, if the original answer was *What time did the clown arrive at the party?* the new answer might be *What time did the boisterous clown in the yellow suit arrive at the party?*)
9. Other students should each show a thumbs-up if they agree that the new answers are more descriptive than the original answer.
10. The student holding the cut-out should set it aside and roll the cube for the rest of the group. If the cube lands on a word that does not correspond to any remaining cut-outs, the student should roll the cube again.
11. The activity continues until all of the cut-outs have been used and all students have taken turns. If desired, shuffle and redistribute the cut-outs and let students continue the activity as time allows.
12. When the activity is complete, store the cut-outs in a resealable plastic bag or a labeled envelope.

who	what	when
where	why	how

What time did _____ arrive at the party?

I met _____ at a basketball tournament.

The _____ was perched on the edge of a steep cliff.

I am saving my money to buy _____ .

I hope to master that new trick by _____ .

_____ , I will start my history project.

Can you give me directions to _____ ?

What kind of fish did you see at _____ ?

Since _____ , our school was closed for the rest of the year!

It was funny to see Katie crawling across the floor because _____ .

Tom will win first prize if _____ .

By _____ , Carol was able to earn enough money to buy a new stereo.

Name: _____ Date: _____

Follow the directions to fill in the blank in each sentence.

1. Fill in the blank with a *who*.

   Did you know that _____ is remarkable?

2. Fill in the blank with a *how*.

   It is easy to paint a picture if you _____ .

3. Fill in the blank with a *where*.

   _____ is in Europe.

✂ ---

Name: _____ Date: _____

Adding Variety Posttest

Follow the directions to fill in the blank in each sentence.

1. Fill in the blank with a *why*.

   I like to play outside because _____ .

2. Fill in the blank with a *what*.

   Can you believe Mark was able to _____ ?

3. Fill in the blank with a *when*.

   I really hope it does not rain _____ .

Programming Instructions

This activity requires students to match root words on cut-outs they are holding to prefixes on cut-outs that are on a cube. Copy and cut apart the Cube Labels (page 79) and the activity cards. Attach each cube label and each activity card to the front of a Colorful Cut-Out™. Attach the cube label cut-outs to the sides of a large, inflatable cube. Or, make a cube using the directions on page 8. Assess students' skill mastery using the Pretest and Posttest (page 81).

Teacher Tip: Laminate the cut-outs and attach them to the cube with removable tape or hook-and-loop tape so that you can store them while using the cube for other activities.

Objective

Students will match prefixes to root words to make new words.

Activity Directions

1. Divide the class into small groups of 3–4 students.
2. Distribute the cut-outs evenly among the groups.
3. Roll the cube for students.
4. Groups should take a moment to look at the root words on their cut-outs and determine which ones form words with the prefix that is showing on the cube.
5. Groups should take turns showing the root words on their cut-outs and sharing the words that they formed. (If desired, write the words on the board or a piece of chart paper.)
6. When all groups have shared their words, have a student roll the cube. If the cube lands on a prefix that has already been used, the student should roll the cube again.
7. The activity continues until all of the prefixes have been used.
8. When the activity is complete, store the cut-outs in a resealable plastic bag or a labeled envelope.

Teacher Note: If desired, prepare the cube and cut-outs for the Suffixes Toss It Activity (pages 82–84) and use the activities at the same time so that students can practice using prefixes and suffixes together. If you choose this option, alternate the two cubes when rolling them.

Answers may include: bicycle, tricycle, bifocal, unclear, uncertain, precook, pretest, submarine, submerge, triangle, tricolor, disappoint, dismount.

bi–   un–   pre–

sub–   tri–   dis–

cycle	focal
clear	certain
cook	test
marine	merge
angle	color
appoint	mount

Name: _____ Date: _____

Fill in each blank with a word from the word bank to make a word with a prefix.

Word Bank				
heat	cycle	clear	honest	merge

1. bi _____

2. pre _____

3. dis _____

4. un _____

✂ -

Name: _____ Date: _____

Fill in each blank with a word from the word bank to make a word with a prefix.

Word Bank				
angle	grace	topic	sure	view

1. sub _____

2. un _____

3. dis _____

4. tri _____

Programming Instructions

This activity requires students to match root words on cut-outs they are holding to suffixes on cut-outs that are on a cube. Copy and cut apart the Cube Labels (page 83) and the activity cards. Attach each cube label and each activity card to the front of a Colorful Cut-Out™. Attach the cube label cut-outs to the sides of a large, inflatable cube. Or, make a cube using the directions on page 8. Assess students' skill mastery using the Pretest and Posttest (page 85).

Teacher Tip: Laminate the cut-outs and attach them to the cube with removable tape or hook-and-loop tape so that you can store them while using the cube for other activities.

Objective

Students will match suffixes to root words to make new words.

Activity Directions

1. Divide the class into small groups of 3–4 students.
2. Distribute the cut-outs evenly among the groups.
3. Roll the cube for students.
4. Groups should take a moment to look at the root words on their cut-outs and determine which ones form words with the suffix that is showing on the cube.
5. Groups should take turns showing the root words on their cut-outs and sharing the words that they formed. (If desired, write the words on the board or a piece of chart paper.)
6. When all groups have shared their words, have a student roll the cube. If the cube lands on a suffix that has already been used, the student should roll the cube again.
7. The activity continues until all of the suffixes have been used.
8. When the activity is complete, store the cut-outs in a resealable plastic bag or a labeled envelope.

Teacher Note: If desired, prepare the cube and cut-outs for the Prefixes Toss It Activity (pages 78–80) and use the activities at the same time so that students can practice using prefixes and suffixes together. If you choose this option, alternate the two cubes when rolling them.
Answers may include: quickest, quickly, kindest, kindly, friendship, friendly, friendless, citizenship, rapidly, boldest, boldly, development, amazement, fearful, fearless, joyful, joyless, thoughtful, thoughtless, careful, careless.

–est | –ship | –ly

–ment | –ful | –less

quick	kind
friend	citizen
rapid	bold
develop	amaze
fear	joy
thought	care

Name: _____ Date: _____

Fill in each blank with a word from the word bank to make a word with a suffix.

Word Bank				
sportsman	young	crazy	curious	amuse

1. _____ment

2. _____est

3. _____ship

4. _____ly

✂ -

Name: _____ Date: _____

Suffixes Posttest

Fill in each blank with a word from the word bank to make a word with a suffix.

Word Bank				
youth	govern	clean	tire	pretty

1. _____est

2. _____ment

3. _____ful

4. _____less

Synonyms

Programming Instructions

This activity requires students to listen to and answer questions about synonyms. Two sets of activity cards have been provided. Each set is labeled with an icon for easy sorting. Select a set of activity cards. (Unlike other activities in this book, the sets of a Search activity cannot be mixed together.) Copy and cut apart the activity cards and attach each one to the front of a Colorful Cut-Out™. Attach the Start Card (page 87 or 88) to the first cut-out. (The cut-out begins with *I know . . . .*) Assess students' skill mastery using the Pretest and Posttest (page 89).

Objective

Students will listen to and answer questions about synonyms.

Activity Directions

1. Shuffle the programmed cut-outs and distribute them to 12 students. (To make this a whole-group activity, have remaining students sit with partners on the floor in front of the 12 students who are holding cut-outs.)
2. Have the student with the start card on his cut-out begin the activity by reading the cut-out aloud. (Remind students to read the cut-outs slowly so that classmates can check their cut-outs. If needed, have students read each cut-out twice before moving to the next cut-out.)
3. Each student with a cut-out should check the first sentence to see if she has the answer. (If the whole class is participating, have students sitting on the floor whisper possible answers to their partners.)
4. The student with the correct answer on his cut-out should read the cut-out aloud.
5. The activity continues until all of the cut-outs have been read aloud. The activity begins and ends with the start card. If desired, shuffle and redistribute the cut-outs for additional skill practice.
6. When the activity is complete, store the cut-outs in a resealable plastic bag or a labeled envelope.

Teacher Note: Each cut-out includes the answer for independent checking. Students should not read these answers aloud. The activity is complete when each cut-out has been read one time.

Synonyms

Start

★ I know synonyms. Who has a synonym for the word *pleasant*?	enjoyable	★ I have *enjoyable*. Who has a synonym for the word *tasty*?	delicious
★ I have *delicious*. Who has a synonym for the word *careful*?	cautious	★ I have *cautious*. Who has a synonym for the word *bold*?	daring
★ I have *daring*. Who has a synonym for the word *surprised*?	shocked	★ I have *shocked*. Who has a synonym for the word *autumn*?	fall
★ I have *fall*. Who has a synonym for the word *foggy*?	hazy	★ I have *hazy*. Who has a synonym for the word *bucket*?	pail
★ I have *pail*. Who has a synonym for the word *dirty*?	filthy	★ I have *filthy*. Who has a synonym for the word *discussion*?	conversation
★ I have *conversation*. Who has a synonym for the word *crazy*?	zany	★ I have *zany*. Who has *I know synonyms*?	Start Card

Synonyms

I know synonyms. Who has a synonym for the word *show*?	display	I have *display*. Who has a synonym for the word *car*?	vehicle
I have *vehicle*. Who has a synonym for the word *brave*?	courageous	I have *courageous*. Who has a synonym for the word *offer*?	volunteer
I have *volunteer*. Who has a synonym for the word *easy*?	simple	I have *simple*. Who has a synonym for the word *walk*?	stroll
I have *stroll*. Who has a synonym for the word *sticky*?	gooey	I have *gooey*. Who has a synonym for the word *active*?	energetic
I have *energetic*. Who has a synonym for the word *succeed*?	accomplish	I have *accomplish*. Who has a synonym for the word *glide*?	soar
I have *soar*. Who has a synonym for the word *contest*?	competition	I have *competition*. Who has *I know synonyms*?	Start Card

Name: _____ Date: _____

Read each word. Fill in the blank with a synonym from the word bank.

Word Bank				
tangy	chatter	sparkling	ooze	sob

1. cry _____

2. talk _____

3. zesty _____

4. glowing _____

- - - ✂ -

Name: _____ Date: _____

Synonyms Posttest

Read each word. Fill in the blank with a synonym from the word bank.

Word Bank				
scurry	thrilled	nosy	conflict	giggle

1. problem _____

2. laugh _____

3. excited _____

4. curious _____

Antonyms

I know antonyms.
Who has an antonym
for the word *guilty*?

| innocent |

I have *innocent*.
Who has an antonym
for the word *smooth*?

| rough |

I have *rough*.
Who has an antonym
for the word *blurry*?

| clear |

I have *clear*.
Who has an antonym
for the word *greedy*?

| generous |

I have *generous*.
Who has an antonym
for the word *laugh*?

| weep |

I have *weep*.
Who has an antonym
for the word *climb*?

| descend |

I have *descend*.
Who has an antonym
for the word *first*?

| last |

I have *last*.
Who has an antonym
for the word *patient*?

| impatient |

I have *impatient*.
Who has an antonym
for the word *timid*?

| fearless |

I have *fearless*.
Who has an antonym
for the word *known*?

| unknown |

I have *unknown*.
Who has an antonym
for the word *peaceful*?

| uneasy |

I have *uneasy*.
Who has *I know
antonyms*?

| Start Card |

Name: _____ Date: _____

Antonyms Pretest

Read each word. Fill in the blank with an antonym from the word bank.

Word Bank				
impossible	lost	less	safe	ending

1. more _____

2. possible _____

3. dangerous _____

4. found _____

- - - ✂ -

Name: _____ Date: _____

Antonyms Posttest

Read each word. Fill in the blank with an antonym from the word bank.

Word Bank				
hollow	laughable	divide	miniature	boring

1. enormous _____

2. multiply _____

3. solid _____

4. serious _____

Compound Words

Programming Instructions

This activity requires students to listen to and answer questions about compound words. Three sets of activity cards have been provided. Each set is labeled with an icon for easy sorting. Select a set of activity cards. (Unlike other activities in this book, the sets of a Search activity cannot be mixed together.) Copy and cut apart the activity cards and attach each one to the front of a Colorful Cut-Out™. Attach the Start Card (page 95, 96, or 97) to the first cut-out. (The cut-out begins with *I know . . . .*) Assess students' skill mastery using the Pretest and Posttest (page 98).

Objective

Students will listen to and answer questions about compound words.

Activity Directions

1. Shuffle the programmed cut-outs and distribute them to 12 students. (To make this a whole-group activity, have remaining students sit with partners on the floor in front of the 12 students who are holding cut-outs.)
2. Have the student with the start card on his cut-out begin the activity by reading the cut-out aloud. (Remind students to read the cut-outs slowly so that classmates can check their cut-outs. If needed, have students read each cut-out twice before moving to the next cut-out.)
3. Each student with a cut-out should check the first sentence to see if she has the answer. (If the whole class is participating, have students sitting on the floor whisper possible answers to their partners.)
4. The student with the correct answer on his cut-out should read the cut-out aloud.
5. The activity continues until all of the cut-outs have been read aloud. The activity begins and ends with the start card. If desired, shuffle and redistribute the cut-outs for additional skill practice.
6. When the activity is complete, store the cut-outs in a resealable plastic bag or a labeled envelope.

Teacher Note: Each cut-out includes the answer for independent checking. Students should not read these answers aloud. The activity is complete when each cut-out has been read one time.

Compound Words

Start

⭐ I know compound words. Who has a compound word with the word *back* in it? | backyard | ⭐ I have *backyard*. Who has a compound word with the word *day* in it? | daylight

⭐ I have *daylight*. Who has a compound word with the word *down* in it? | downstairs | ⭐ I have *downstairs*. Who has a compound word with the word *every* in it? | everyone

⭐ I have *everyone*. Who has a compound word with the word *water* in it? | waterslide | ⭐ I have *waterslide*. Who has a compound word with the word *rain* in it? | rainfall

⭐ I have *rainfall*. Who has a compound word with the word *rise* in it? | sunrise | ⭐ I have *sunrise*. Who has a compound word with the word *ball* in it? | basketball

⭐ I have *basketball*. Who has a compound word with the word *dog* in it? | bulldog | ⭐ I have *bulldog*. Who has a compound word with the word *cat* in it? | wildcat

⭐ I have *wildcat*. Who has a compound word with the word *milk* in it? | buttermilk | ⭐ I have *buttermilk*. Who has *I know compound words*? | Start Card

Name: _____ Date: _____

Fill in each blank with a word from the word bank to make a compound word.

Word Bank

foot	thunder	mail	boat	fish

1. air _____

2. gold_____

3. bare _____

4. _____storm

✂ -

Name: _____ Date: _____

Fill in each blank with a word from the word bank to make a compound word.

Word Bank

end	rain	wind	touch	case

1. suit _____

2. week_____

3. _____mill

4. _____down

Programming Instructions

This activity requires students to listen to and answer questions about the definitions of words. Two levels of activity cards have been provided. The levels increase in difficulty from the Apprentice Level (page 100) to the Expert Level (page 101). Select an activity level. (Unlike other activities in this book, the levels of a Search activity cannot be mixed together.) Copy and cut apart the activity cards and attach each one to the front of a Colorful Cut-Out™. Attach the Start Card (page 100 or 101) to the first cut-out. (The cut-out begins with *I know . . . .*) Assess students' skill mastery using the Pretest and Posttest (page 102).

Objective

Students will listen to and answer questions about the definitions of words.

Activity Directions

1. Shuffle the programmed cut-outs and distribute them to 12 students. (To make this a whole-group activity, have remaining students sit with partners on the floor in front of the 12 students who are holding cut-outs.)

2. Have the student with the start card on her cut-out begin the activity by reading the cut-out aloud. (Remind students to read the cut-outs slowly so that classmates can check their cut-outs. If needed, have students read each cut-out twice before moving to the next cut-out.)

3. Each student with a cut-out should check the first sentence to see if she has the answer. (If the whole class is participating, have students sitting on the floor whisper possible answers to their partners.)

4. The student with the correct answer on her cut-out should read the cut-out aloud.

5. The activity continues until all of the cut-outs have been read aloud. The activity begins and ends with the start card. If desired, shuffle and redistribute the cut-outs for additional skill practice.

6. When the activity is complete, store the cut-outs in a resealable plastic bag or a labeled envelope.

Teacher Note: Each cut-out includes the answer for independent checking. Students should not read these answers aloud. The activity is complete when each cut-out has been read one time.

I know definitions. Who has a word that means *a structure that goes over a river*?

bridge

I have *bridge*. Who has a word that means *a dry region*?

desert

I have *desert*. Who has a word that means *a young deer*?

fawn

I have *fawn*. Who has a word that means *the final course of a meal*?

dessert

I have *dessert*. Who has a word that means *newly made, not stale*?

fresh

I have *fresh*. Who has a word that means *a position of work*?

job

I have *job*. Who has a word that means *a device for securing a door*?

lock

I have *lock*. Who has a word that means *to say no*?

refuse

I have *refuse*. Who has a word that means *to guide the direction of a car*?

steer

I have *steer*. Who has a word that means *to pull apart*?

tear

I have *tear*. Who has a word that means *a fee paid to cross a bridge*?

toll

I have *toll*. Who has *I know definitions*?

Start Card

What Does It Mean?

EXPERT

Start

I know definitions. Who has a word that means *to growl*?	snarl	I have *snarl*. Who has a word that means *to have a strong effect on someone*?	impress
I have *impress*. Who has a word that means *to trap something*?	snare	I have *snare*. Who has a word that means *to shake with fear*?	tremble
I have *tremble*. Who has a word that means *to become weary*?	tire	I have *tire*. Who has a word that means *to go down*?	descend
I have *descend*. Who has a word that means *a quick look*?	glimpse	I have *glimpse*. Who has a word that means *often*?	frequent
I have *frequent*. Who has a word that means *to talk*?	converse	I have *converse*. Who has a word that means *money paid as a penalty*?	fine
I have *fine*. Who has a word that means *to fool or mislead*?	bluff	I have *bluff*. Who has *I know definitions*?	Start Card

Blended Words

I know invented words. Who has a word that combines *clap* and *crash*?	clash	I have *clash*. Who has a word that combines *motor* and *hotel*?	motel
I have *motel*. Who has a word that combines *breakfast* and *lunch*?	brunch	I have *brunch*. Who has a word that combines *squirm* and *wriggle*?	squiggle
I have *squiggle*. Who has a word that combines *flutter* and *hurry*?	flurry	I have *flurry*. Who has a word that combines *splash* and *spatter*?	splatter
I have *splatter*. Who has a word that combines *twist* and *whirl*?	twirl	I have *twirl*. Who has a word that combines *gleam* and *shimmer*?	glimmer
I have *glimmer*. Who has a word that combines *smoke* and *fog*?	smog	I have *smog*. Who has a word that combines *slop* and *slush*?	slosh
I have *slosh*. Who has a word that combines *smack* and *mash*?	smash	I have *smash*. Who has *I know invented words*?	Start Card

Name: _____ Date: _____

Read each pair of words. Fill in the blank with a word from the word bank that combines the two words.

Word Bank				
flush	flurry	clump	motel	flare

1. chunk + lump = _____

2. flame + glare = _____

3. flash + gush = _____

4. motor + hotel = _____

- - - ✂ -

Name: _____ Date: _____

Read each pair of words. Fill in the blank with a word from the word bank that combines the two words.

Word Bank				
moped	brunch	because	mash	blotch

1. blot + botch = _____

2. breakfast + lunch = _____

3. by + cause = _____

4. motor + pedal = _____

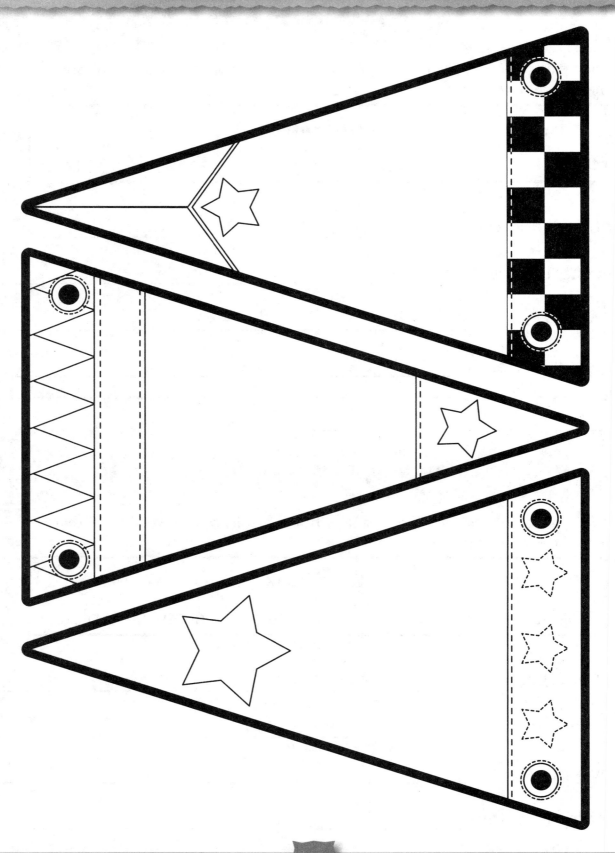

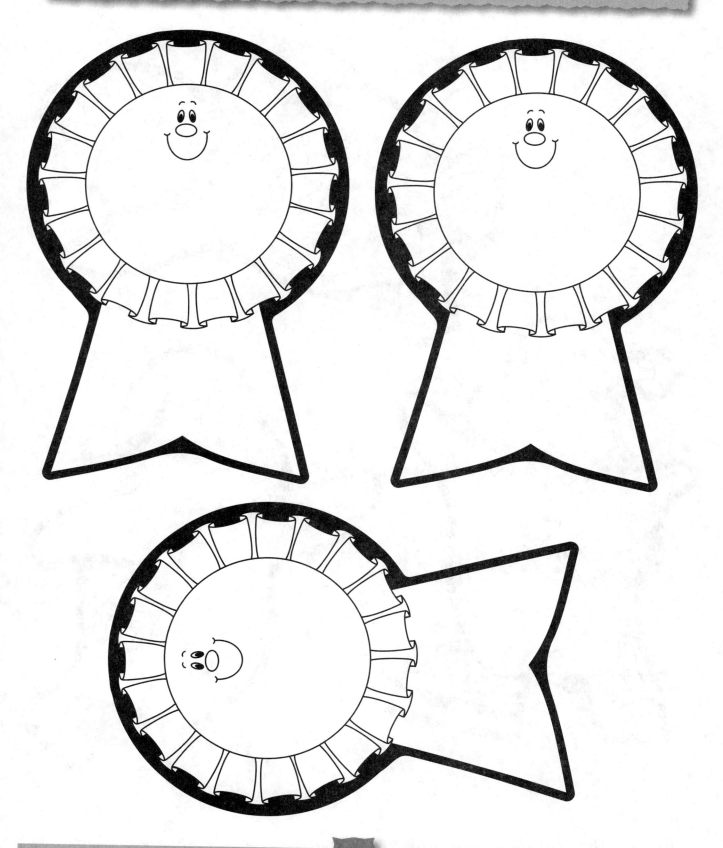

Answer Key

Words That Sound the Same
page 16
PRETEST
1. knows
   Sentences will vary.
2. week
   Sentences will vary.
POSTTEST
1. waste
   Sentences will vary.
2. tale
   Sentences will vary.

What Does Not Belong?
page 20
PRETEST
1. ocean; not in the sky
2. snake; not an insect
3. sister; not a male family member
POSTTEST
1. rooster; not a baby animal
2. chicken; does not have four legs
3. shark; does not have a shell

More Than One Meaning
page 24
PRETEST
1. saw   2. squash
3. swallow   4. light
POSTTEST
1. tick   2. mole
3. leave   4. well

Using Verb Tenses
page 28
PRETEST
Sentences will vary but should use the following verbs:
1. bake or bakes
2. baked
3. will bake
POSTTEST
Sentences will vary but should use the following verbs:
1. take or takes
2. took
3. will take

Solving Analogies
page 32
PRETEST
1. uncle   2. happy
3. crying   4. brush
POSTTEST
1. forget   2. whisper
3. reptile   4. carpenter

Editing for Conventions
page 41
PRETEST

1. the math marathon will be a fantastic event for everyone

2. do you think the competition will start on time? asked Margaret.

3. Wow! Our class did a great job planning setting up and hosting

POSTTEST

1. I can't believe the math marathon was so close! exclaimed Marcus.

2. "I know," said Victoria. Do you think everyone had fun?

3. it seemed like everyone had a fabulous time said miss jackson

Sentence Roundup
page 45
PRETEST
1. a.   2. c.   3. b.
POSTTEST
1. b.   2. a.   3. c.

Answer Key

Counting Syllables
page 50
PRETEST
1. b. 2. a. 3. b.
4. c. 5. b. 6. d.
POSTTEST
1. d. 2. c. 3. b.
4. b. 5. c. 6. d.

How Do You Spell the Plural?
page 54
PRETEST
1. videos 2. bodies
3. selves 4. women
POSTTEST
1. heroes 2. calves
3. countries 4. sandboxes

Focus on Word Choice
page 58
PRETEST
Answers will vary.
POSTTEST
Answers will vary.

Be an Expert:
Alphabetical Order
page 63
PRETEST
1. lemon, monkey, mouth
2. door, duck, dust
3. vicious, victory, violin
POSTTEST
1. barnyard, basket, cheesecake
2. feather, ferret, firewood
3. element, elephant, elevator

Be an Expert:
It's a Noun and a Verb
page 67
PRETEST
Answers will vary.
POSTTEST
Answers will vary.

Adding Variety
page 77
PRETEST
Answers will vary.
POSTTEST
Answers will vary.

Prefixes
page 81
PRETEST
1. bicycle 2. preheat
3. dishonest 4. unclear
POSTTEST
1. subtopic 2. unsure
3. disgrace 4. triangle

Suffixes
page 85
PRETEST
1. amusement
2. youngest
3. sportsmanship
4. curiously
POSTTEST
1. cleanest 2. government
3. youthful 4. tireless

Synonyms
page 89
PRETEST
1. sob 2. chatter
3. tangy 4. sparkling
POSTTEST
1. conflict 2. giggle
3. thrilled 4. nosy

Antonyms
page 93
PRETEST
1. less 2. impossible
3. safe 4. lost
POSTTEST
1. miniature 2. divide
3. hollow 4. laughable

Compound Words
page 98
PRETEST
1. airmail 2. goldfish
3. barefoot 4. thunderstorm
POSTTEST
1. suitcase 2. weekend
3. windmill 4. touchdown

What Does It Mean?
page 102
PRETEST
1. drowsy 2. gesture
3. brochure 4. active
POSTTEST
1. schedule 2. flexible
3. scramble 4. rigid

Blended Words
page 105
PRETEST
1. clump 2. flare
3. flush 4. motel
POSTTEST
1. blotch 2. brunch
3. because 4. moped

Programming Instructions

This activity requires students to listen to statements and determine whether they are facts or opinions. Cut apart the preprinted Colorful Cut-Outs™ (inside back cover).

Objective

Students will listen to statements and determine whether they are facts or opinions.

Activity Directions

1. Shuffle the programmed cut-outs.
2. Have 10 students sit in a circle on the floor.
3. Give each student a cut-out with the activity card facedown. (The text should not be visible.) Instruct students not to look at the fronts of the cut-outs.
4. Give a signal for students to start quickly passing the cut-outs around the circle. Each student should be holding only one cut-out at a time.
5. At the signal, students should stop passing the cut-outs and look at the fronts of the cut-outs they are holding.
6. Choose one student to read the challenge on her cut-out aloud to the whole group.
7. Each student should take a moment to think about the challenge and whisper his answer to a neighbor.
8. The student to the left of the student who is holding the cut-out should answer aloud.
9. Other students should each show a thumbs-up if they agree. The student holding the cut-out should confirm the correct answer and then put her cut-out aside.
10. The student to her left who answered the challenge should now read his cut-out aloud to the group.
11. The activity continues until all of the cut-outs have been used or all students have taken turns leading the group.
12. When the activity is complete, store the cut-outs in a resealable plastic bag or a labeled envelope.

Teacher Note: If desired, have students offer ways to change opinion statements to factual statements.